T0353929

TIME ZONES

THIRD EDITION

NICHOLAS BEARE

NATIONAL
GEOGRAPHIC
LEARNING

Australia · Brazil · Canada · Mexico · Singapore · United Kingdom · United States

National Geographic Learning,
a Cengage Company

Time Zones Starter Combo Third Edition
Nicholas Beare

Publisher: Andrew Robinson

Executive Editor: Sean Bermingham

Managing Editor: Derek Mackrell

Development Editor: Kirsty Hine

Director of Global Marketing: Ian Martin

Senior Product Marketing Manager: Anders Bylund

Heads of Regional Marketing:
    Charlotte Ellis (Europe, Middle East and Africa)
    Kiel Hamm (Asia)
    Irina Pereyra (Latin America)

Senior Production Controller: Tan Jin Hock

Associate Media Researcher: Jeffrey Millies

Senior Designer: Lisa Trager

Operations Support: Rebecca G. Barbush,
    Hayley Chwazik-Gee

Manufacturing Planner: Mary Beth Hennebury

Composition: Symmetry Creative Productions, Inc.

© 2021 Cengage Learning, Inc.

WCN: 01-100-371

ALL RIGHTS RESERVED. No part of this work covered by the copyright herein may be reproduced or distributed in any form or by any means, except as permitted by U.S. copyright law, without the prior written permission of the copyright owner.

"National Geographic", "National Geographic Society" and the Yellow Border Design are registered trademarks of the National Geographic Society ® Marcas Registradas

For permission to use material from this text or product, submit all requests online at **cengage.com/permissions** Further permissions questions can be emailed to **permissionrequest@cengage.com**

Student's Book Combo with the Spark platform
ISBN-13: 978-0-357-42172-7

Student's Book Combo
ISBN-13: 978-0-357-41894-9

National Geographic Learning
5191 Natorp Boulevard
Mason, OH 45040
USA

Locate your local office at **international.cengage.com/region**

Visit National Geographic Learning online at **ELTNGL.com**
Visit our corporate website at **www.cengage.com**

Printed in the United States of America
Print Number: 06   Print Year: 2024

CONTENTS

SCOPE AND SEQUENCE

UNIT	FUNCTIONS	GRAMMAR	VOCABULARY	PRONUNCIATION	READ, WRITE, & WATCH
1 HELLO!					PAGE 8
	Saying hello and goodbye Asking people's names Talking about your family **Real English:** *See you later!*	**Am / Is / Are:** *I'm, you're, she's, he's* **Singular possessive adjectives:** *my, your, his, her* **Possessive 's:** *Maya's*	Greetings Family members Classroom items	Contractions *I'm, you're, he's, she's*	**Reading:** My Family **Writing:** Describe Your Family **Video:** Families
2 WHERE ARE YOU FROM?					PAGE 20
	Talking about countries and nationalities Describing colors Describing country flags **Real English:** *How about you?*	**Using *where* and *from*:** *Where are you from? I'm from Brazil.* **Plural possessive adjectives:** *our, your, their* **Using *what* and color:** *What color is it? It's red.*	Countries, nationalities, and continents Colors Sport	*a* and *an*	**Reading:** Naomi Osaka **Writing:** A Famous Person **Video:** A Fast Race
3 WHAT'S THAT?					PAGE 32
	Talking about animals Counting from 1 to 12 Talking about singular and plural things **Real English:** *Oh no!*	**Using demonstratives:** *What's this? What's that?* *What are these? What are those?* **Indefinite articles:** *a* and *an* **Singular and plural nouns:** *cat, cats, pen, pens*	Animals Irregular plurals Numbers 1 to 12	Final *s* sounds	**Reading:** Amazing Chameleons **Writing:** An Animal Poster **Video:** The National Geographic Photo Ark
4 IT'S A CELEBRATION!					PAGE 44
	Learning the months of the year Learning numbers 13 to 100 Talking about special days **Real English:** *Happy birthday!*	**Talking about dates and ages:** *How old are you? I'm 15 years old.* *What's the date?* *When's your birthday?* *It's August 5th.* *What month is it? It's February.*	Seasons Numbers 11 to 100 Ordinal numbers	*th* sounds	**Reading:** *Hanami* **Writing:** Special Day **Video:** Festival of Colors
5 MY HOME					PAGE 56
	Talking about the rooms in a house Asking and saying where things are **Real English:** *Here she is!*	**Using *where* and *in*:** *Where is the dog?* *It's in the yard.* *Is the dog in the yard?* *Yes it is. No it isn't*	Rooms in a home Body parts	Linking words	**Reading:** A Tiny House **Writing:** Descriptive Paragraph **Video:** Strange Houses
6 WHAT TIME IS IT?					PAGE 68
	Learning the days of the week Telling the time **Real English:** *What's up?*	**Expressions of time:** *It's 8 o'clock.* *It's ten o eight.* *It's 6 p.m.* *Good morning. Good afternoon.* *Good evening. Good night.*	Expressions of time Times of day Days of the week	*ng* sounds	**Reading:** A Special Clock **Writing:** City Guide **Video:** Around the World

MEET THE *TIME ZONES* TEAM

MAYA

MING

STIG

NADINE

This is **Maya Santos** from Rio de Janeiro, in Brazil. She's into music, singing, and shopping.

This is **Ming Chen** from Shanghai, in China. He likes sports and animals.

This is **Stig Andersson** from Stockholm, in Sweden. He loves food, photography, and sports.

This is **Nadine Barnard** from Cape Town, in South Africa. She loves nature, movies, and music.

GETTING STARTED

Teacher Language

Open your books.

Turn to page 6.

Read the text aloud.

Close your books.

Write a sentence.

Raise your hand.

Work with a partner.

Work in groups.

Student Language

Asking and answering questions

Can you repeat that, please? / Thank you.

What does "repeat" mean? / It means "say it again."

How do you say "…" in English?

What's this? / It's a pen.

What are these? / They're notebooks.

Working in pairs and groups

Are you ready? / Just a minute.

You go first. / I'll go first.

What do you have for number 1? / I have "computer."

I'm A, you're B.

Let's do it again.

What do we do next?

1 HELLO!

PREVIEW

A 🎧 **1.1 Look at the photo and listen.** Circle the names.

1 Her name is **Mrs. Sato** / **Mrs. Tanaka**.

2 His name is **Ken** / **Mark**.

B 🎧 **1.2 Listen.** Circle the names.

1 He's **Mike** / **Chris**.

  She's **Mia** / **Sofia**.

2 Her name is **Emily** / **Pamela**.

  His name is **John** / **José**.

A woman greets tourists at a Japanese inn.

Talk with a partner. Say hello.

Hi. My name's Lucy.

Hello, Lucy. I'm Fred.

UNIT GOALS

- say hello and goodbye

- learn how to ask people's names

- talk about your family

LANGUAGE FOCUS

A 🎧 **1.3** **Listen and read.** Talk with a partner. Say hello and goodbye.

> REAL ENGLISH See you later!

Stig:	Hello.
Nadine:	Hi, I'm Nadine.
Stig:	How do you spell that?
Nadine:	N-A-D-I-N-E. What's your name?
Stig:	My name's Stig.
Nadine:	How do you spell that?
Stig:	T-H-A-T. Ha ha! No, it's S-T-I-G.
Ming:	Bye, Maya.
Maya:	See you later, Ming!

B 🎧 **1.4** **Look at the chart.** Then match.

AM / IS / ARE (TO *BE* SINGULAR)	
I'm Stig. **You're** Nadine.	
She's Maya. **He's** Ming.	
HIS / HER / YOUR / MY (POSSESSIVE ADJECTIVES)	
What's **your** name?	**My** name is Stig.
What's **his** name? What's **her** name?	**His** name is Ming. **Her** name is Maya.
What's **my** name?	**Your** name is Nadine.
'S (POSSESSIVE S)	
Maya**'s** family name is Santos.	

1 I ○   ○ are ('re)
2 She ○   ○ am ('m)
3 You ○   ○ is ('s)

C 🎧 1.5 **Listen and repeat.**

ALPHABET						
Aa	Bb	Cc	Dd	Ee	Ff	Gg
Hh	Ii	Jj	Kk	Ll	Mm	Nn
Oo	Pp	Qq	Rr	Ss	Tt	Uu
Vv	Ww	Xx	Yy	Zz		

CAPITAL LETTERS

Capital letters ⟨ Stig / Maya / Nadine

D 🎧 1.6 **Listen and write their names.**

1 _____   3 _____

2 _____   4 _____

E **Work with a partner.** Write a list of people in your class.

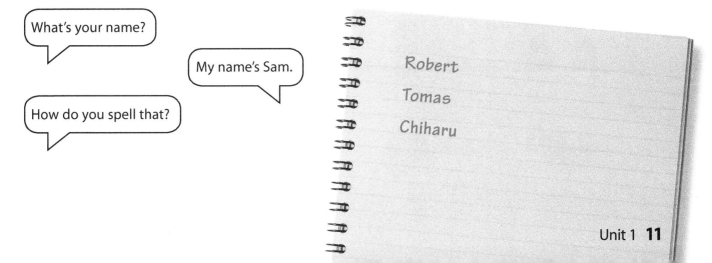

What's your name?

My name's Sam.

How do you spell that?

Robert
Tomas
Chiharu

THE REAL WORLD

GREETINGS

Two girls hug to say hello at a high school in New Jersey, USA.

A 🎧 **1.7** **Match the parts of the conversation.** Listen and check. Then practice with a partner.

Hi, my name's Ahmed.	○	○ See you later.
Nice to meet you, Sarah.	○	○ Hi, I'm Sarah.
Bye, Sarah.	○	○ It's nice to meet you too, Ahmed.

B ▶ **1.1** **Watch the video.** Match.

bow   hug   kiss   shake hands   wave   fist bump

1 _____

3 _____

5 _____

2 _____

4 _____

6 _____

C Talk with a partner. How do you greet someone?

> I wave and smile.

PRONUNCIATION *contractions*

🎧 1.8 **Listen.** Circle the words you hear. Then listen again and repeat.

1 **I am** / **I'm** Simon.

2 **She is** / **She's** Sofia.

3 **He is** / **He's** Ken.

4 **You are** / **You're** Daniela.

COMMUNICATION

Talk with a partner. Say hello and goodbye. Use a greeting from **B** on page 12.

> Hi. My name's Maria.

> Hello, Maria. Nice to meet you. I'm Wei.

> Bye, Wei!

> See you, Maria!

Two young men in Germany fist bump to say hello.

READING

A **Look at the photo.** What can you see?

☐ a family   ☐ a house   ☐ a car

B **Read the article.** <u>Underline</u> the names.

Sarah and her family

MY FAMILY

🎧 **1.9** Here is my **family**. My name is Sarah. My **brother** is Andy. I'm his **sister**.

My **mom's** name is Heidi. My **dad's** name is Peter.

COMPREHENSION

A   Read *My Family* and complete the chart.

PICTURE	NAME
	Sarah

B   Work with a partner. Ask about the photo.

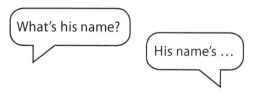

What's his name?

His name's …

VOCABULARY

A **Find these words in** *My Family.* **Then match the labels below.**

dad   brother   sister   mom

1 my _____   4 _____

2 _____ *me* _____   5 _____

3 _____   6 _____

B   Look at the illustration. Then label the pictures.

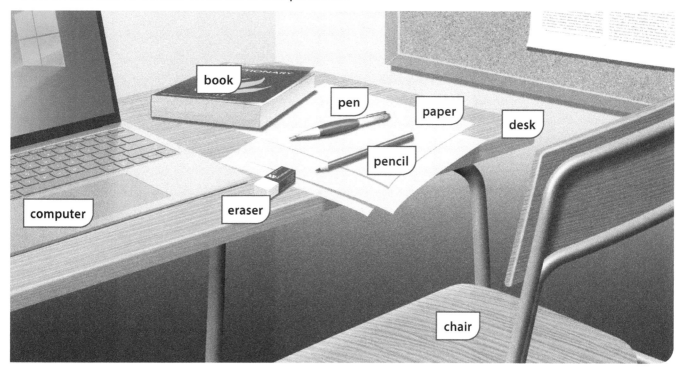

1 _____   3 _____   5 _____   7 _____

2 _____   4 _____   6 _____   8 _____

WRITING

A   Look at the photo and read the paragraph.

B   Think about your family. Write your names.

C   Write a paragraph about your family.

My name is Ramon. My mom is Paula. My dad ....

FAMILIES

Before You Watch

Look at the photo. Who do you see?

☐ sisters　　　☐ brothers　　　☐ dad　　　☐ mom

While You Watch

A ▶ 1.2 **Watch the video.** Circle the correct answers.

1 Ana has a **dad** / **mom**.

2 Sonia has a **sister** / **brother**.

B ▶ 1.2 **Watch again.** Are these sentences true (**T**) or false (**F**).

1 Ana has a brother.　　　　　　　**T**　　**F**

2 Sonia's mom's name is Veena.　　**T**　　**F**

3 Josh's brother's name is Sanjeet.　**T**　　**F**

4 Josh has sisters.　　　　　　　　**T**　　**F**

After You Watch

Talk with a partner. Talk about your family.

Ana and her family.

A Circle the correct words.

1 His name **is** / **are** John.

2 She **is** / **are** my sister

3 **A:** What **is** / **are** your name?

   B: My name **is** / **are** Mary.

4 How do you **say** / **spell** that?

5 **Ming's** / **Ming is** last name is Chen.

B Label the people in the family.

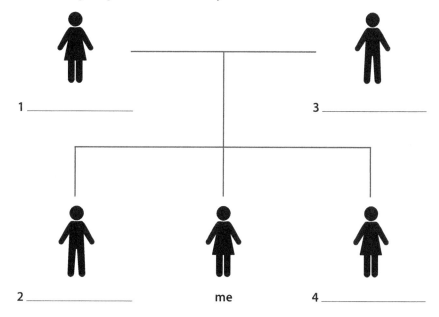

1 _____

3 _____

2 _____

me

4 _____

C Label the pictures.

1 _____ 2 _____ 3 _____ 4 _____

SELF CHECK   Now I can …

☐ say hello and goodbye

☐ ask someone's name

☐ talk about my family.

WHERE ARE YOU FROM?

Flags at the 1984 Olympic Games in Los Angeles, USA

PREVIEW

A 🎧 **2.1 Listen.** Match the colors.

1	⬜ ○	○	brown
2	⬜ ○	○	red
3	⬜ ○	○	yellow
4	⬜ ○	○	pink
5	⬜ ○	○	purple
6	⬛ ○	○	white
7	⬜ ○	○	blue
8	⬜ ○	○	black
9	⬜ ○	○	green
10	○	○	orange

B **Talk with a partner.** What colors are in the photo?

C **Talk with a partner.** Find the colors in your classroom.

> The board is white.

> Yes, and my pen is blue.

PEOPLE AND PLACES

UNIT GOALS
• talk about countries and nationalities

• learn about colors

• find out about country flags

LANGUAGE FOCUS

A 🎧 **2.2** **Listen and read.** Is Nadine from Sweden? Then repeat the conversation and replace the words in **bold**.

> **REAL ENGLISH** How about you?

Nadine:	Hi, Ming. Hi, Stig. Where are you from? Are you from the US?
Ming:	No, we're not from the US. I'm from China.
Stig:	And I'm from **Stockholm**. (**Bangkok / Lima**)
Nadine:	Where's that?
Stig:	It's in **Sweden**. (**Thailand / Peru**)
Nadine:	How about Maya? Where's she from?
Ming:	She's from **Sao Paulo**. **Sao Paulo** is in **Brazil**. (**Seoul**, **Korea / Paris**, **France**)
Stig:	How about you? Where are you from?
Nadine:	I'm from South Africa.
Ming:	Is that in Asia?
Nadine:	No, South Africa is in Africa, of course!

B 🎧 **2.3** **Look at the chart.** Then circle the correct answers below.

TALKING ABOUT YOUR COUNTRY (USING *FROM* AND NATIONALITIES)		
Where are you **from**?	I'm **from**	Brazil. I'm Brazilian.
Where's he **from**?	He's **from**	Japan. He's Japanese.
Where are you **from**?	We're **from**	The United States. We're American.
Where are they **from**?	They're **from**	Korea. They're Korean.
OUR / YOUR / THEIR (POSSESSIVE ADJECTIVES)		
Our / Your / Their	names are	Nadine and Maya.
ASKING ABOUT COLORS		
What color is it?	It's green / red / blue.	

1 We say, "I'm + **country / nationality**."

2 We say, "I'm from + **country / nationality**."

3 We say, "It's **black / black color**."

C 🎧 2.4 **Listen and complete the information.** Then talk with a partner. Where are you from?

1

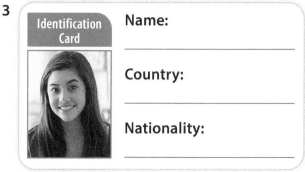

Identification Card

Name: _____

Country: _____

Nationality: _____
          Brazilian

3

Identification Card

Name: _____

Country: _____

Nationality: _____

2

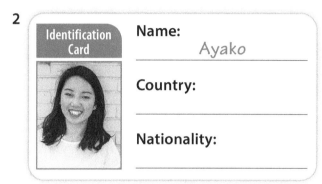

Identification Card

Name: _____
          Ayako

Country: _____

Nationality: _____

4

Identification Card

Name: _____

Country: _____
          Turkey

Nationality: _____

D **Look at the picture below.** Number the colors.

~~brown~~   ~~red~~   pink   purple   white   blue   black   green   orange

1 _____

2 _____

3 _____

4 _____

5 _____

6 _____

7 ___brown___

8 ___red___

9 _____

E **Talk with a partner.** Ask and answer questions about the photo.

What color is this?

It's red.

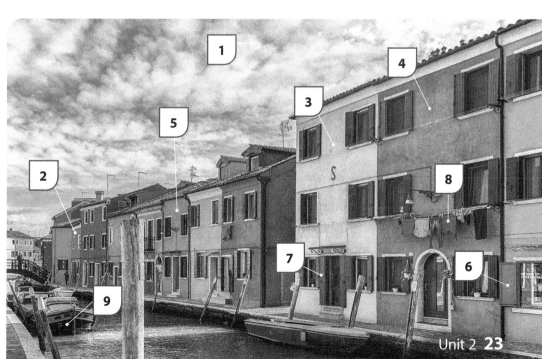

Colorful buildings in Burano, Italy

FLAGS

Flags from countries in North America and South America

A **Complete the labels.** What colors are the flags?

1 Jamaica's flag is green, _____, and _____.

3 The United Kingdom's flag is white, _____, and _____.

2 Australia's flag is red, _____, and _____.

4 Colombia's flag is _____, _____, and _____.

B ▶ **2.1** **Watch the video.** Match the countries to the flags.

South Korea	Ireland	Mexico	South Africa

1 _____ 2 _____ 3 _____ 4 _____

C **Talk with a partner.** What color is your country's flag?

PRONUNCIATION *a and an*

A 🎧 **2.5** **Listen and write *a* or *an*.**

1 _____ chair

2 _____ eraser

3 _____ desk

4 _____ orange pen

B **Work in pairs.** Say the words.

COMMUNICATION Make a class flag.

A **Work in pairs.** Draw a flag for your class.

B **Talk about your flag.** Tell another pair about your flag.

Our flag is green, blue, and yellow.

READING

A **Look at the photo.** Naomi Osaka
is a _____ .

   a   soccer player

   b   tennis player

   c   golf player

B **Talk with a partner.** Where is
Naomi Osaka from?

Naomi OSAKA

🎧 **2.6** Naomi Osaka is a Japanese tennis **player**. She is
very **strong**—she hits the **ball** at 200 kilometers per hour.
That is very **fast**. She was **the winner** of the US Open in
2018 and the Australian Open in 2019. In 2019, she was
5 the number one woman player in **the world**.

Naomi's father is Leonard. He is from Haiti. Her mother is
from Japan. Her name is Tamaki. Naomi's sister is a tennis
player, too. Her name is Mari, and she is Japanese. Naomi
speaks English and Japanese.

Naomi Osaka at the 2019 Porsche Grand Prix in Stuttgart, Germany

COMPREHENSION

A Answer the questions about *Naomi Osaka*.

1 MAIN IDEA What is the article mainly about?

a a strong tennis player

b tennis in Japan

c women tennis players

2 DETAIL Where is Naomi's father from?

a Japan   b Australia   c Haiti

3 DETAIL Naomi's sister's name is _____ .

a Leonard   b Mari   c Tamaki

4 REFERENCE In line 8, *she* means _____ .

a Tamaki   b Naomi   c Mari

B Talk with a partner. Who are some athletes from your country?

VOCABULARY

A **Find the words below in _Naomi Osaka_.** Then label the pictures.

player   strong   ball   fast   the winner   the world

1 _____   3 _____   5 _____

2 soccer _____   4 _____   6 _____

B 🎧 **2.7 Listen.** Number the continents on the map (**1–7**).

1 ~~Asia~~   **2** Europe   **3** Australia   **4** North America   **5** Africa   **6** Antarctica   **7** South America

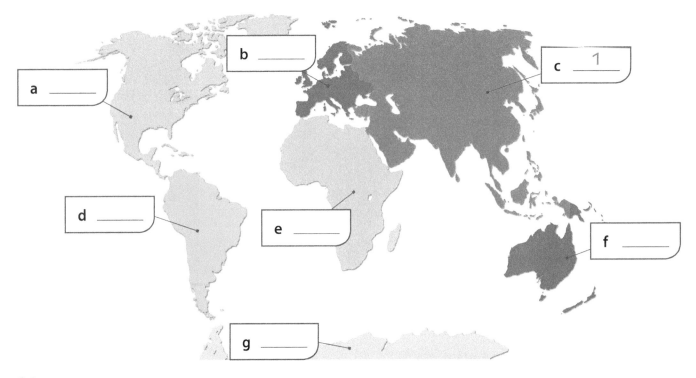

C Label the continents.

1 _____Asia_____

5 _____

2 _____

6 _____

3 _____

7 _____

4 _____

WRITING

A Look at the photo and read the paragraph.

B Choose a famous person or someone you know. Make notes about his or her family. Where is he or she from?

C Write about the person.

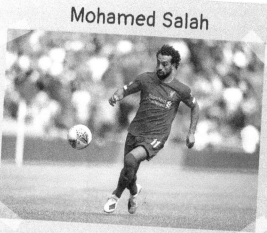

Mohamed Salah

Mohamed Salah is from Egypt. He is a very good soccer player...

A *FAST* **RACE**

Before You Watch

Talk with a partner. Look at the photo. What are their names? Who do you think is the winner?

While You Watch

A ▶ 2.2 **Watch the video.** Match the runners to the countries.

1 Bolt ○   ○ the Netherlands

2 Martina ○   ○ Jamaica

3 Bailey ○   ○ Brazil

4 Moreira ○   ○ the United States

B ▶ 2.2 **Watch again.** Answer the questions.

1 Where is this race?

   a China   b Brazil   c Italy

2 Who is the winner?

   a Martina   b Bolt   c Bailey

After You Watch

Talk with a partner. Are you a fast runner?

Bolt and Bailey in a 100-meter race

A Write the colors.

1 _____

2 _____

3 _____

4 _____

5 _____

6 _____

7 _____

8 _____

B Circle the correct words.

1 I'm from **Mexico** / **Mexican**.

2 She's **American** / **the United States**.

3 They're **Turkey** / **Turkish**.

4 We're from **the United Kingdom** / **British**.

C Rearrange the letters to make continents.

1 h r t o N e r i m a A c   _____

2 u o p E r e   _____

3 a i A s   _____

4 h t o S u r m A c e i a   _____

5 r a i f A c   _____

6 l s u a i a A t r   _____

7 t a c t a n i A c r   _____

SELF CHECK   Now I can ...

☐ talk about countries and nationalities

☐ talk about colors

☐ talk about country flags

WHAT'S
THAT?

A baby lemur in a zoo in Florida, USA

PREVIEW

A **3.1** **Listen.** Write the animals you hear.

rabbit   fish   dog   bird   mouse   cat

1 _____ 3 _____ 5 _____

2 _____ 4 _____ 6 _____

B **3.2** **Listen and match.**

1 cat	○	○	black
2 dog	○	○	white
3 mouse	○	○	brown
4 fish	○	○	blue
5 bird	○	○	orange
6 rabbit	○	○	yellow

C **Talk with a partner.** What pet do you like?

I like cats.

Me too!

THE NATURAL WORLD

UNIT GOALS

• learn about some amazing animals

• count from 1 to 12

• talk about singular and plural things

LANGUAGE FOCUS

A 🎧 **3.3 Listen and read.** What is on Nadine? Then repeat the conversation and replace the words in **bold**.

REAL ENGLISH Oh no!

Nadine: Look at the animals!

Maya: They're **amazing**! (**great** / **so cool**)

Nadine: What's that?

Maya: It's a bear.

Nadine: And what are those?

Maya: They're monkeys.

Maya: Nadine, what's that?

Nadine: Where?

Maya: On **you**! (**your arm** / **your shirt**)

Nadine: Oh no! It's a spider!

B 🎧 **3.4 Look at the chart.** Then circle the correct answers below.

THIS / THAT / THESE / THOSE (DEMONSTRATIVES)			
What's this?	**It's** a dog.	**What are these?**	**They're** cats.
What's that?	**It's** a spider.	**What are those?**	**They're** rabbits.
A / AN (ARTICLES)			
a cat		**an** eraser	
SINGULAR AND PLURAL			
cat		cat**s**	
pen		pen**s**	

1 *This* and *that* are for **one** / **more than one** thing.

2 *These* and *those* are for **one** / **more than one** thing.

3 *This* and *these* are for **here** / **over there** and *that* and *those* are for **here** / **over there**.

C Circle the correct word.

1 **This** / **These** are dogs.

2 **That** / **Those** are his pens.

3 **That** / **Those** is my desk.

4 What's **this** / **those**?

D Complete the questions and answers.

1 **A:** What are _____ these _____ ?

   B: _____ They're _____ parrots.

2 **A:** What are _____ ?

   B: _____ lions.

3 **A:** What's _____ ?

   B: _____ a turtle.

4 **A:** What's _____ ?

   B: _____ an elephant.

E Talk with a partner. Use *this*, *that*, *these*, and *those* to talk about things in your classroom.

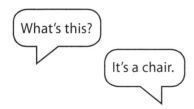

What's this?

It's a chair.

IDIOM

"He's as quiet as _____."
a a cat
b a mouse
c a fish

Unit 3 **35**

COUNTING ANIMALS

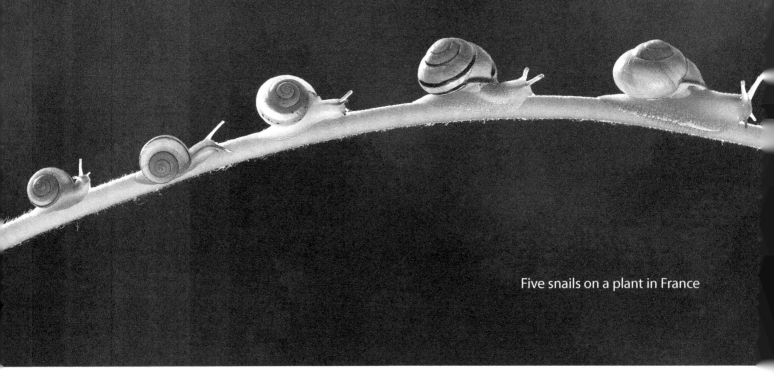

Five snails on a plant in France

A 🎧 **3.5** **Listen and repeat.**

0	1	2	3	4	5	6
zero	one	two	three	four	five	six

7	8	9	10	11	12	
seven	eight	nine	ten	eleven	twelve	

B 🎧 **3.6 Listen.** Circle the correct number.

a 11	6	4		**g** 2	0	9
b 5	10	6		**h** 1	8	10
c 7	4	9		**i** 8	9	7
d 8	10	4		**j** 2	1	6
e 9	2	7		**k** 11	9	5
f 7	12	1		**l** 3	8	0

DO YOU KNOW?

Which animal lives on land and in the water?
a a duck
b a shark
c a bear

C ▶ **3.1 Watch the video.** Match the number with the animal. Then say the answers to your partner.

1 ○ ○ lizards	**5** ○ ○ snails	**9** ○ ○ ladybugs
2 ○ ○ birds	**6** ○ ○ lions	**10** ○ ○ sheep
3 ○ ○ dogs	**7** ○ ○ fish	**11** ○ ○ cats
4 ○ ○ rabbit	**8** ○ ○ monkeys	**12** ○ ○ cows

PRONUNCIATION *s/z* plurals

A 🎧 **3.7 Listen.** Circle the sound you hear.

1 s   z   **2** s   z   **3** s   z   **4** s   z

B **Work with a partner.** Read the words below to your partner.

pens   cats   dogs   books   rabbits   cows

COMMUNICATION

Talk with a partner. Student A: Say your telephone number. **Student B:** Repeat the number.

My phone number is zero two four five …

Is your phone number zero two four five … ?

READING

A **Look at the photo.** A chameleon is a _____ .

☐ lizard   ☐ bird   ☐ fish

B **Talk with a partner.** What colors can you see?

A chameleon on a tree branch
in Madagascar

AMAZING CHAMELEONS

🎧 **3.8** Chameleons are a kind of lizard. There are a lot of different chameleons. Many are from Madagascar. They live in **trees**.

Chameleons are red, green, blue, and other colors. They
5 can **change** color to communicate with other chameleons. Chameleons **eat** insects. Their **tongues** are very **long**. Chameleon's **eyes** are special. They can look at two different things. One eye can look up and one eye can look down.

COMPREHENSION

A Answer the questions about *Amazing Chameleons*.

1 MAIN IDEA What is this article about?

    a an animal

    b insects

    c a country in Africa

2 DETAIL Where are many chameleons from?

    a Australia   **b** Peru   **c** Madagascar

3 DETAIL Chameleons can change their _____.

    a tongue   **b** eyes   **c** color

4 REFERENCE In line 7, *they* refers to _____.

    a a chameleon's eyes

    b things

    c colors

B Talk with a partner. Do you like chameleons? Are they a good pet?

VOCABULARY

A **Find these words in *Amazing Chameleons*.** Then complete the labels.

trees   change   eat   tongue   long   eyes

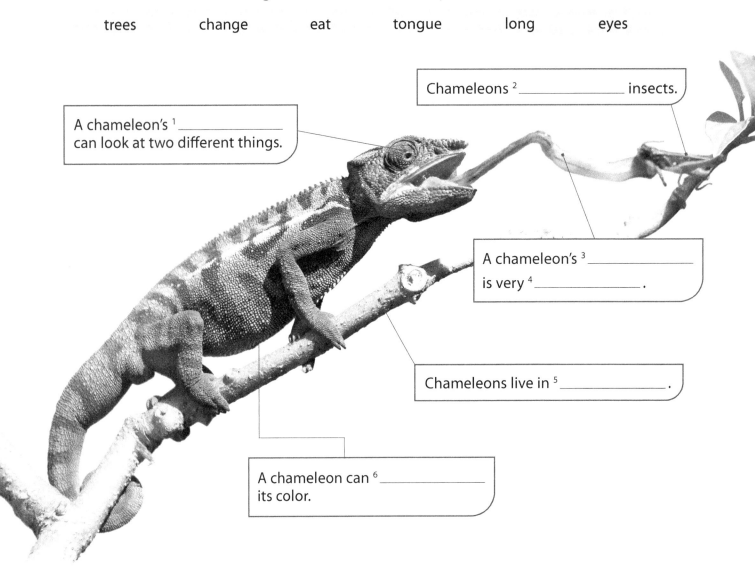

Chameleons ² _____ insects.

A chameleon's ¹ _____
can look at two different things.

A chameleon's ³ _____
is very ⁴ _____.

Chameleons live in ⁵ _____.

A chameleon can ⁶ _____
its color.

B **Look at the information below.** Then label the photos on page 41.

Irregular Plurals

Most plurals use **s**. For example: cat → cat**s**, book → book**s**
Irregular plurals are different:

Singular	Plural
man	men
woman	women
child	children
mouse	mice
sheep	sheep
fish	fish

1 two sheep

4 _____

2 _____

5 _____

3 _____

6 _____

Giraffes

This is a giraffe. Giraffes are from Africa. They are yellow and brown. Their necks are very long …

WRITING

A Look at the photo and read the poster.

B Choose an animal. Find a photo of the animal. Make notes about the animal. Use a dictionary.

C Make a poster. Write about your animal. Use your notes from **B**.

THE NATIONAL GEOGRAPHIC PHOTO ARK

Before You Watch

Look at the photo. What does Joel Sartore take photos of?

a animals   b people   c flowers

While You Watch

A   ▶ 3.2   **Watch the video.** Are these sentences true (**T**) or false (**F**)

1	Joel Sartore takes photos at zoos.	T	F
2	The animals are pets.	T	F
3	Other people help Joel.	T	F
4	Joel's job is very difficult.	T	F

B   ▶ 3.2   **Watch again.** Write the names of three animals you see.

After You Watch

Talk with a partner. Do you want Joel Sartore's job?

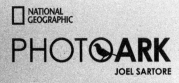

Joel Sartore photographs a caiman at a zoo in Kansas, USA.

A   **Label the animals.**

1 _____   4 _____

2 _____   5 _____

3 _____   6 _____

B   **Circle the answer.**

1   **This** / **These** are dogs.   3   **That** / **Those** are his pens.

2   **That** / **Those** is my desk.   4   What's **this** / **those**?

C   **Write the correct word.**

Singular	Plural
mouse	*mice*
fish	
sheep	
man	
woman	
child	

SELF CHECK   Now I can ...

☐ talk about animals
☐ count from 1 to 12
☐ talk about singular and plural things

4

IT'S A
CELEBRATION!

A girl celebrates at a party for her 15th birthday.

PREVIEW

A 🎧 **4.1 Listen and match.**

gift candles cake card party balloon

1 _____ 4 _____

2 _____ 5 _____

3 _____ 6 _____

B Talk with a partner. Ask and answer questions about the photo.

What's that?

It's a birthday cake.

What color is it?

It's white.

HISTORY AND CULTURE

UNIT GOALS

- learn the months of the year
- learn numbers from 13 to 100
- talk about some special days

LANGUAGE FOCUS

A 🎧 **4.2** **Listen and read.** Is it Stig's birthday? Then repeat the conversation and replace the words in **bold**.

> **REAL ENGLISH** Happy birthday!

Stig: What's that?

Maya: It's a **cake**, of course! (**gift** / **card**)

Stig: Is it a birthday **cake**? (**gift** / **card**)

Maya: Yes it is. It's for you. Happy birthday, Stig!

Stig: It's not my birthday!

Ming: But it's **July 13th**. Isn't your birthday today?
(**August 6th** / **March 9th**)

Stig: No, my birthday's on **July 30th**!
(**August 16th** / **March 19th**)

B 🎧 **4.3** **Look at the chart.** Then look at **C** and **D** on page 47 and write the answers below.

TALKING ABOUT DATES AND AGES	
How old are you?	I'm 15 years old.
How old is he?	He's 32 years old.
He isn't 25 years old. It isn't his birthday.	
What's the date?	It's August 5th.
When's your birthday?	It's January 8th.
What month is it?	It's January / February / March …

1 How old are you? _____

2 How old is your mom (or dad)? _____

3 When is your birthday? _____

C 🎧 **4.4** **Listen and repeat the names of the months.**

2019	JANUARY	FEBRUARY	MARCH	APRIL	MAY	JUNE
	S M T W T F S	S M T W T F S	S M T W T F S	S M T W T F S	S M T W T F S	S M T W T F S
	1 2 3 4 5	1 2	1 2	1 2 3 4 5 6	1 2 3 4	1
	6 7 8 9 10 11 12	3 4 5 6 7 8 9	3 4 5 6 7 8 9	7 8 9 10 11 12 13	5 6 7 8 9 10 11	2 3 4 5 6 7 8
	13 14 15 16 17 18 19	10 11 12 13 14 15 16	10 11 12 13 14 15 16	14 15 16 17 18 19 20	12 13 14 15 16 17 18	9 10 11 12 13 14 15
	20 21 22 23 24 25 26	17 18 19 20 21 22 23	17 18 19 20 21 22 23	21 22 23 24 25 26 27	19 20 21 22 23 24 25	16 17 18 19 20 21 22
	27 28 29 30 31	24 25 26 27 28	24 25 26 27 28 29 30 31	28 29 30	26 27 28 29 30 31	23 24 25 26 27 28 29 30

	JULY	AUGUST	SEPTEMBER	OCTOBER	NOVEMBER	DECEMBER
	S M T W T F S	S M T W T F S	S M T W T F S	S M T W T F S	S M T W T F S	S M T W T F S
	1 2 3 4 5 6	1 2 3	1 2 3 4 5 6 7	1 2 3 4 5	1 2	1 2 3 4 5 6 7
	7 8 9 10 11 12 13	4 5 6 7 8 9 10	8 9 10 11 12 13 14	6 7 8 9 10 11 12	3 4 5 6 7 8 9	8 9 10 11 12 13 14
	14 15 16 17 18 19 20	11 12 13 14 15 16 17	15 16 17 18 19 20 21	13 14 15 16 17 18 19	10 11 12 13 14 15 16	15 16 17 18 19 20 21
	21 22 23 24 25 26 27	18 19 20 21 22 23 24	22 23 24 25 26 27 28	20 21 22 23 24 25 26	17 18 19 20 21 22 23	22 23 24 25 26 27 28
	28 29 30 31	25 26 27 28 29 30 31	29 30	27 28 29 30 31	24 25 26 27 28 29 30	29 30 31

D 🎧 **4.5** **Listen and repeat.**

11	eleven	20	twenty	29	twenty-nine
12	twelve	21	twenty-one	30	thirty
13	thirteen	22	twenty-two	40	forty
14	fourteen	23	twenty-three	50	fifty
15	fifteen	24	twenty-four	60	sixty
16	sixteen	25	twenty-five	70	seventy
17	seventeen	26	twenty-six	80	eighty
18	eighteen	27	twenty-seven	90	ninety
19	nineteen	28	twenty-eight	100	a hundred

E 🎧 **4.6** **Listen.** Write the numbers you hear.

a _____twelve_____   d _____   g _____

b _____   e _____   h _____

c _____   f _____

F **Play a game. Student A:** Think of a number between 10 and 100. **Student B:** Guess Student A's number.

20?

Higher.

25?

Lower.

23?

That's right!

THE REAL WORLD

SEASONS

Fall colors in Argentina

A 🎧 **4.7 Listen and match.** Write the seasons.

| fall | spring | summer | winter |

      ◎

1 _____   2 _____   3 _____   4 _____

B ▶ **4.1 Watch the video.** Complete the chart with the seasons.

Country	March to May	June to August	September to November	December to February
South Korea	spring			winter
Argentina	fall		spring	

C **Work with a partner.** Look at the chart. Talk about the seasons in the two countries.

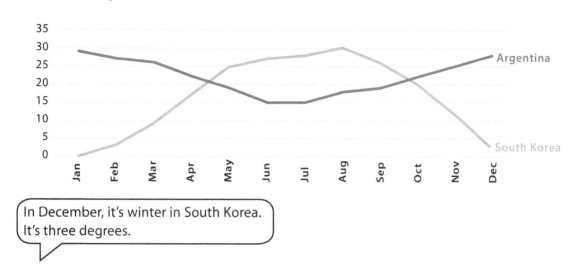

In December, it's winter in South Korea. It's three degrees.

PRONUNCIATION *th* sounds

🎧 **4.8** **Listen and repeat.** Then say the words to a partner.

think   three   both   with   this   that   mother   father

COMMUNICATION

A **Look at the photo.** Choose one person. Complete the information.

B **Role play.** Look at the photo and choose a person. Fill in the blanks for that person. Ask and answer questions with a partner. Then choose another person and role play again.

Me: My name is _____ .

I'm _____ years old.

My birthday is _____ .

My country: I'm from _____ .

In my country it is _____ .

It is _____ degrees .

What's your name?

My name is …

Where are you from?

I'm from …

Every spring, people in Japan enjoy *hanami*.

READING

A Look at the photo. Hanami is a _____ festival.

☐ spring   ☐ fall   ☐ winter

B Talk with a partner. What can you see at a hanami festival?

HANAMI

🎧 **4.9** Every spring, people in Japan enjoy a special **festival**. The festival is *hanami*. It's Japan's cherry blossom festival (a *blossom* is a **flower**). *Hanami* is in March, April, or May.

5 People meet their friends in a city **park**. They put a large **blanket** on the **ground**. Then they sit on the blanket and enjoy a **picnic**. People like to sit under the cherry trees and look at the beautiful pink blossoms.

Hanami is popular in other countries, too. In
10 Washington D.C. in the United States, many people like to celebrate *hanami*.

COMPREHENSION

A Answer the questions about *Hanami*. Circle **T** for true or **F** for false.

1 Hanami is in July or August.	**T**	**F**
2 Friends sit on the ground and have a picnic.	**T**	**F**
3 Cherry blossoms are green.	**T**	**F**
4 Many countries enjoy hanami.	**T**	**F**

B Talk with a partner. What festivals are popular in your country?

VOCABULARY

A Find these words in *Hanami*. Write the words under the pictures.

festival   flower   park   blanket   ground   picnic

1 _____   2 _____   3 _____

4 _____   5 _____   6 _____

B 🎧 4.10 Listen and write the numbers.

tenth   fourteenth   seventeenth   twenty-second   twenty-ninth   twenty-sixth
nineteenth   fifteenth   twenty-seventh   eighth   sixth   twenty-third

1st	first	11th	eleventh	21st	twenty-first
2nd	second	12th	twelfth	22nd	_____
3rd	third	13th	thirteenth	23rd	_____
4th	fourth	14th	_____	24th	twenty-fourth
5th	fifth	15th	_____	25th	twenty-fifth
6th	_____	16th	sixteenth	26th	_____
7th	seventh	17th	_____	27th	_____
8th	_____	18th	eighteenth	28th	twenty-eighth
9th	ninth	19th	_____	29th	_____
10th	_____	20th	twentieth	30th	thirtieth

Ordinal Numbers

first   → 1st   third   → 3rd
second → 2nd   fourth → 4th

C Look at the calendar. Then complete the sentences below.

May 1st
May Day

May 10th
Mothers' Day
in Mexico

May 5th
Children's Day
in Japan

May 28th
Hamburger Day
in Australia

May

Monday	Tuesday	Wednesday	Thursday	Friday	Saturday	Sunday
1	2	3	4	5	6	7
8	9	10	11	12	13	14
15	16	17	18	19	20	21
22	23	24	25	26	27	28
29	30	31				

1 May Day is on May _____1st_____.

2 Children's Day in _____ is on May _____.

3 Mother's Day in _____ is on _____.

4 Hamburger Day in Australia is on _____.

WRITING

A Look at the photo and read the paragraph.

B Think about a special day in your country or city. Make notes about it. Find a photo.

C Write about a special day in your country. Use your notes from **B**.

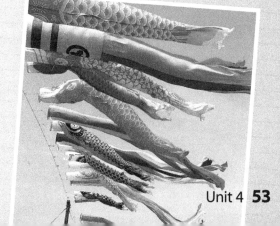

Children's Day is a special day
in Japan. It's on May 5th.

FESTIVAL OF **COLORS**

Before You Watch

Look at the photo. What country is this? What colors do you see?

While You Watch

A   ▶ 4.2 **Watch the video.** Check (✓) the things you see.

☐ colorful powder   ☐ people dancing   ☐ Indian sweets

B   ▶ 4.2 **Watch again.** Check (✓) the sentences that are true about Holi.

_____ Holi is in July or August.

_____ People throw colorful powder.

_____ People eat special sweets.

_____ People enjoy dancing at Holi.

After You Watch

Talk with a partner. Do you want to go to the Holi festival?

Holi is a special festival in India.

A Write the numbers in words.

a 31 _thirty-one_   f 72 _____

b 23 _____   g 59 _____

c 64 _____   h 45 _____

d 90 _____   i 48 _____

e 17 _____   j 86 _____

B Circle the correct answers.

1 How **old** / **age** are you?

2 **A:** What **day** / **month** is it?

   B: It's June.

3 **A:** What's the **day** / **date**?

   B: It's January 9th.

4 **A:** What **month** / **season** is it in New Zealand?

   B: It's winter there now.

C Complete the sentences.

1 August is the ____eighth____ month.

2 June is the _____ month.

3 _____ is the tenth month.

4 _____ is the third month.

5 December is the _____ month.

SELF CHECK   Now I can …

☐ talk about dates

☐ count from 13 to 100

☐ talk about some special days

5

MY **HOME**

PREVIEW

A 🎧 **5.1** **Listen and match.** Where do you find these things?

bathroom   dining room   living room
bedroom   kitchen   yard

1 The plant is in the

_____

4 The bed is in the

_____

2 The bath is in the

_____

5 The pot is in the

_____

3 The TV is in the

_____

6 The table is in the

_____

B **Talk with a partner.** What rooms do you see in the photo?

C **Talk with a partner.** What is in your house?

> My bed is in my bedroom.

> A TV is in my living room.

PEOPLE AND PLACES

UNIT GOALS

• talk about the rooms in a house

• ask and say where things are

• find out about some interesting houses

LANGUAGE FOCUS

A 🎧 **5.2 Listen and read.** Where is Nadine's cat? Then repeat the conversation and replace the words in **bold**.

> **REAL ENGLISH** Here she is!

Maya:	Where's your cat today?
Nadine:	I don't know. Is she in the **yard**? (**living room / bathroom**)
Maya:	No, she isn't. Is she in the kitchen?
Nadine:	No, she isn't.
Maya:	Maybe she's in the bedroom.
Nadine:	No, I don't think so.
Maya:	Oh! Here she is. She's **under the bed**! (**in the closet / on the bed**)

B 🎧 **5.3 Look at the chart.** Then circle the correct answers below.

TALKING ABOUT WHERE THINGS ARE (USING THE VERB *BE* WITH *WHERE* AND *IN*)	
Where is the dog? **Where are** the books?	**He is in** the yard. **They're in** the living room.
Is the dog **in** the yard?	Yes, he **is**. No, he **isn't**.
Are the books **in** the kitchen?	Yes, they **are**. No, they **aren't**.

1 *Where* is for questions about **time / place**.

2 For talking about rooms, we say **in / on** the room.

C 🎧 **5.4 Look at the picture below.** Complete the questions and answers. Then listen to check.

1 Where's Robert? _____ in the _____.

2 Where's Jenny? _____ in the _____.

3 _____ Bella? _____.

4 _____ Simon? _____.

5 _____ the books? _____.

D **Look at the picture below.** Complete the questions and answers.

1 Is the cat in the yard? No, _____.

2 _____ the dog _____ yard? Yes, _____.

3 Are the books in the bedroom? _____.

4 _____ Simon _____ bathroom? _____.

5 _____ pen in the bedroom? _____.

E **Talk with a partner.** Ask and answer questions about the picture.

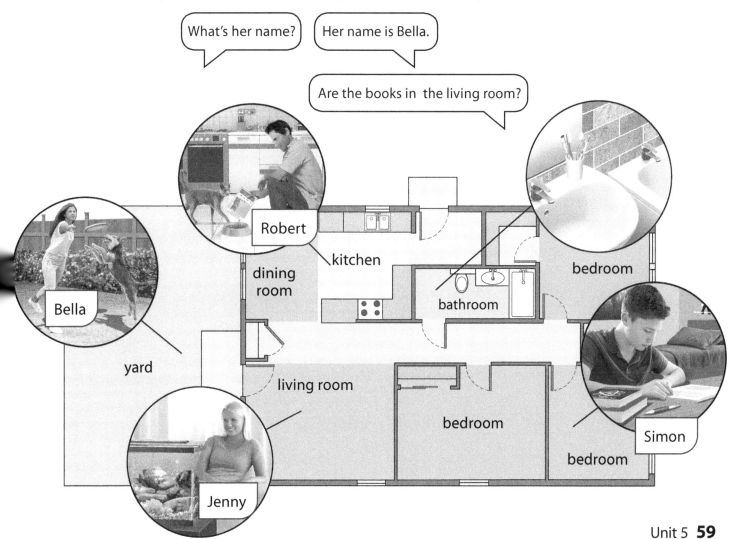

What's her name?

Her name is Bella.

Are the books in the living room?

Robert

kitchen

dining room

bathroom

bedroom

Bella

yard

living room

bedroom

Simon

Jenny

bedroom

THE REAL WORLD

DINOSAUR IN THE ROOM

A fossil of a dinosaur's head is in this family's living room.

A Look at the photo and read the caption. What do you see? Talk with a partner.

> Two children are in the living room.

B ▶ 5.1 Watch the video. Where is each room? Match the places.

  a London, UK   **b** Milan, Italy   **c** Boston, USA

1 _____

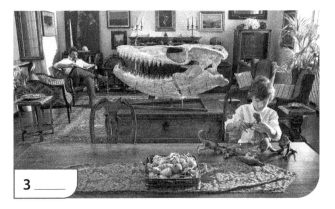

3 _____

2 _____

C ▶ **5.1** **Watch again.** Complete the sentences.

1 There are **four** / **six** children in the first photo.

2 The fossil in the first photo is **brown** / **white**.

3 The dinosaur in the second photo is on the **ground** / **ceiling**.

4 The dinosaur in the second photo is very **long** / **small**.

5 The fossil in the third photo is on a **table** / **chair**.

6 The boy in the last photo is with his **mom** / **dad**.

PRONUNCIATION linking

🎧 **5.5** **Listen.** Draw a line to connect the linked sounds. Then say the sentences to a partner.

1 It's in the living room.

2 He's in the kitchen.

3 They're on the bed.

4 She's in the yard.

COMMUNICATION

Draw a floor plan of your house. Talk with a partner about your house.

> This is the kitchen. This is my bedroom. My bed is in my bedroom.

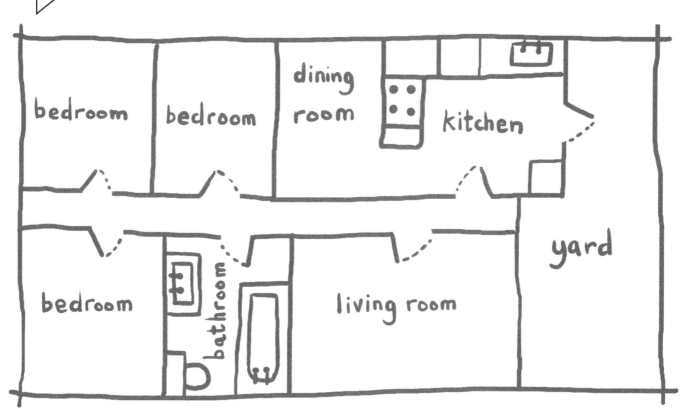

READING

A **Look at the photo.** What can you see in this house? Make a list.

B **Skim the article.** <u>Underline</u> some things you can find in this house.

The Pinafore is very small inside.

A TINY HOUSE

🎧 **5.6** Welcome to a **tiny** house! The name of this house is the Pinafore. The living room is very small. Two **cushions** are on the **couch**. Some books are in the living room, too. A **stove** is in the small kitchen.

5 A computer is on the kitchen table. A big **window** is in the living room.

The bed is up the **stairs**. The bed is very small, too. The Pinafore is tiny. It's only seven meters long, and two meters wide. But it is cheap and easy to live in.

COMPREHENSION

A Answer the questions about *A Tiny House*.
Circle **T** for true or **F** for false.

1 A bed is in the Pinafore.   T   F

2 The couch is up the stairs.   T   F

3 The Pinafore is about three meters long. T   F

4 Some books are in the living room.   T   F

B Design your tiny house. Draw a picture. Show it to your partner.

> The kitchen is small. It is in the living room.

Zyl Vardos makes tiny houses. This is the Pinafore.

VOCABULARY

A **Find the words below in *A Tiny House*.** Then label the photo using the words in the box.

cushion   couch   stove   window   stairs

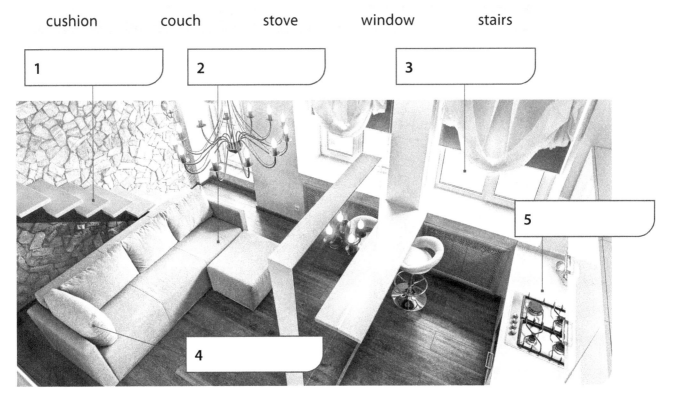

1
2
3
5
4

B 🎧 **5.7** **Listen and repeat.** Label the parts of the body in the photo.

ear   leg   hair   foot   mouth   eye   arm   hand   ~~head~~   nose

1   head
2
3
4
5
6
7
8
9
10

C Label the two photos below. Write parts of the body.

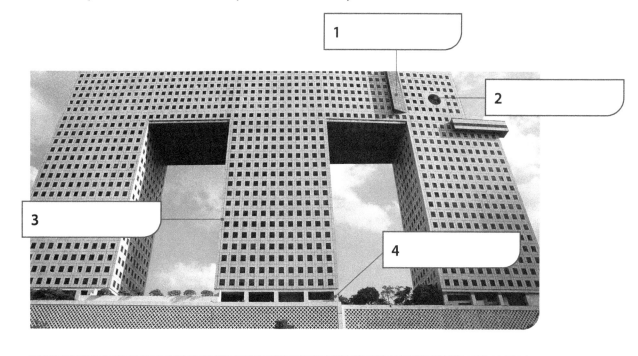

1

2

3

4

5

6

WRITING

A Look at the photo and read the paragraph.

B Make notes about your house. What rooms are in your house? What is in each room?

C Write about your house. Use your notes from **B**.

My house is small. It is an apartment. A couch and some cushions are in the living room ...

STRANGE HOUSES

Before You Watch

Look at the photo at the bottom of the page. Why is this house strange?

While You Watch

A ▶ 5.2 **Watch the video.** Circle the answers.

1 a **fruit** / **rock** house

3 a **seashell** / **shoe** house

5 a **rock** / **shoe** house

2 a **tree** / **glass bottle** house

4 **an upside-down /
a seashell** house

Germany

6 an **airplane** / **dinosaur** house

B ▶ 5.2 **Watch again.** Where is each house? Write the country.

Canada   ~~Germany~~   Mexico   Portugal   South Africa   the United States

After You Watch

Talk with a partner. Which house do
you like best?

This house in France
looks like a spaceship.

A Rearrange the letters to make rooms.

1 o m r a t h o b   _____

2 d a y r   _____

3 c n h t e i k   _____

4 g i v n i l o m o r   _____

5 o d b o e m r   _____

B Rearrange the words to make questions and answers.

1 **A:** pen / where's / your _____?

   B: on / it's / table / the _____.

2 **A:** in / is / kitchen / stove / the / the _____?

   B: is / it / yes, _____.

3 **A:** are / books / the / where _____?

   B: bedroom / in / my / they're _____.

C Label the body parts.

| arm | ear | foot | hand | leg | nose |

1 _____   3 _____   5 _____

2 _____   4 _____   6 _____

SELF CHECK   Now I can …

- [ ] talk about the rooms in a house
- [ ] ask and say where things are
- [ ] talk about some interesting houses

6

WHAT **TIME** IS IT?

24 hours in one photo in New York, the United States

PREVIEW

A 🎧 **6.1 Listen and match.**

afternoon   day   evening   morning   night

 7:00 AM

 2:00 PM

1 _____   4 _____

7:00 PM

 12:00 PM

2 _____   5 _____

1:00 AM

3 _____

B 🎧 **6.2 Listen. Where is this place?**

a   New York, the United States

b   Bangkok, Thailand

c   Buenos Aires, Argentina

d   Venice, Italy

C   Talk with a partner. What times of day in **A** can you see in the picture?

> This is morning.

> Yes, and this is afternoon.

PEOPLE AND PLACES

UNIT GOALS

• learn the days of the week

• tell the time

• find out about places at different times

LANGUAGE FOCUS

A 🎧 **6.3 Listen and read.** What time is it in Sweden? Then repeat the conversation and replace the words in **bold**.

REAL ENGLISH   What's up?

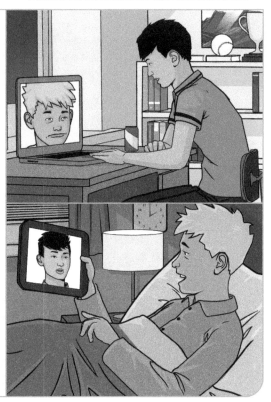

Stig: Hello?

Ming: Good morning, Stig! **What's up?** (**How are you?** / **How's it going?**)

Stig: I'm really tired! What time is it?

Ming: It's **9 o'clock** in China. It's morning. (**8 o'clock** / **10 o'clock**)

Ming: Where are you?

Stig: I'm at home.

Ming: What time is it?

Stig: It's **2 o'clock** in Sweden! I'm in bed! (**1 o'clock** / **3 o'clock**)

B 🎧 **6.4 Look at the chart.** Then circle the correct answers below.

TALKING ABOUT TIME AND DAYS	
What time is it?	It's 8 o'clock. (8:00) It's nine thirty. (9:30) It's eight forty-five. (8:45) It's ten oh eight. (10:08) It's 10 a.m. (10:00) It's 6 p.m. (6:00)
Good morning. / Good afternoon. / Good evening. / Good night.	

1 At 10:00 we say, "**It's ten zero zero** / **It's ten o'clock**."

2 At 11:05 we say, "**It's eleven oh five** / **It's eleven zero five**."

3 Nine a.m. is in the **morning** / **afternoon**.

C 🎧 6.5 **What time is it?** Write the times. Then listen and check.

1 _Ten twenty-five_   3 _____   5 _____

2 _____   4 _____   6 _____

D Match the times and expressions.

1 It's 9:15 a.m. ○   ○ Good evening.
2 It's 3:00 p.m. ○   ○ Good night.
3 It's 6:30 p.m. ○   ○ Good morning.
4 It's 11:00 p.m. ○   ○ Good afternoon.

E Talk with a partner. Ask and answer questions about the time.

What time is it?

It's nine fifteen.

Good morning!

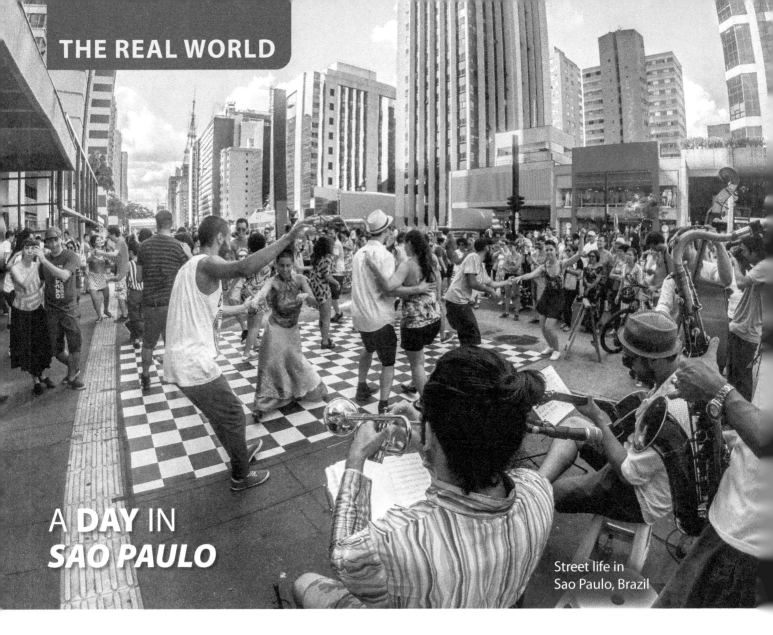

THE REAL WORLD

A **DAY** IN
SAO PAULO

Street life in
Sao Paulo, Brazil

A 🎧 **6.6** **Take a quiz.** Then listen and check your answers.

1 Sao Paulo is in _____ .

   a Mexico   **b** Portugal   **c** Brazil

2 _____ people are in Sao Paulo.

   a 3 million   **b** 6 million   **c** 12 million

3 Winter in Sao Paulo is from _____ .

   a March to May   **b** June to August   **c** December to February

Big Numbers

   1,000 = 1 thousand

   1,000,000 = 1 million

   1,000,000,000 = 1 billion

B ▶ **6.1** **Watch the video.** Write *morning, afternoon, evening,* or *night.*

a _____

c _____

b _____

d _____

PRONUNCIATION *ng* sound

🎧 **6.7** **Listen and repeat.** Then say the words to a partner.

1 thing
2 morning

3 evening
4 song

5 king
6 ring

COMMUNICATION

A **Write the times.** Choose nine times of day from the box. Write them in the bingo chart below.

2:20	4:10	10:05	9:30	6:15	6:50
3:05	6:45	9:10	2:25	10:40	11:55

B **Work with a partner.** Play time bingo. Ask the time and cross off the times your partner says. The first student with three in a row wins.

What time is it?

It's two twenty-five.

BINGO

Example:

BINGO		
4:10	9:30	3:05
9:10	2:20	2:25
11:55	10:40	6:15

The Glockenspiel is very popular with tourists.

READING

A Look at the photos. Where is this?

   a Italy   **b** Germany   **c** Mexico

B Talk with a partner. What can you see in the two photos?

A SPECIAL CLOCK

🎧 **6.8** In the **city** of Munich, Germany, there is a very special clock. It's more than 100 years old. Many **tourists** come to see—and hear—this amazing **clock**.

The name of the clock is the Glockenspiel (GLOCK-en-
5 shpeel). Forty-three **bells** are in the clock. Every day, at 11 a.m. and 12 p.m. the bells ring. Thirty-two **models** of animals and people come out. Some dance. Some are on horses. In 15 minutes the models go back inside. The **show** ends. It starts again at the same time tomorrow.

COMPREHENSION

A Answer the questions about *A Special Clock*.

  1 MAIN IDEA What is the Glockenspiel?

    a a model   **b** a clock   **c** a bell

  2 DETAIL How old is the clock?

    a 32 years old

    b 42 years old

    c more than 100 years old

  3 DETAIL How many bells are in the clock?

    a 32   **b** 43   **c** 100

  4 DETAIL How long is the show?

    a 5 minutes

    b 15 minutes

    c 30 minutes

B Talk with a partner. What is special about the Glockenspiel?

VOCABULARY

A **Find these words in *A Special Clock*.** Write the words under the pictures.

city   ~~tourists~~   clock   bell   model   a show

1 _____

4   *tourists* _____

2 _____

5 _____

3 _____

6 _____

B 🎧 **6.9 Look at the calendar.** Then listen and complete the days of the week.

November

Monday	Tuesday	Wednesday	Thursday	Friday	Saturday	Sunday
1	2	3	4	5	6	7
8	9	10	11	12	13	14
15	16	17	18	19	20	21
22	23	24	25	26	27	28
29	30					

1 M __o__ __n__ d __a__ y

2 T u ____ ____ d ____ y

3 ____ e d ____ ____ s d ____ ____

4 T h u ____ ____ ____ ____ y

5 ____ r ____ d ____ y

6 ____ ____ ____ u r ____ a ____

7 S ____ n d ____ y

I'm from Istanbul. Istanbul is a big city. It's in Turkey ...

WRITING

A Look at the photo and read the paragraph.

B Think about your city. What is special? What is good for tourists? Make a list.

C Write about your city. Use your notes from **B.**

AROUND THE WORLD

Before You Watch

Talk with a partner. Look at the list of countries. What continent is each country in?

China is in Asia.

While You Watch

A ▶ 6.2 **Watch the video.** Number the countries in order.

	Country	Time
	China	
	the United Kingdom	
	Kenya	
1	Peru	6:00 a.m.
	India	
	the United States	
	Australia	

B ▶ 6.2 **Watch again.** Write the time in each place.

After You Watch

Talk with a partner. What time is it now in your town or city? What time is it now in the places above?

Early morning in
Machu Picchu, Peru

A Match the times.

1 6:45 a.m.   ○   ○   afternoon

2 1:37 p.m.   ○   ○   evening

3 6:30 p.m.   ○   ○   night

4 1:00 a.m.   ○   ○   morning

B Write the times.

1 _six forty-five_

3 _____

2 _____

4 _____

C Unscramble the days of the week.

1 s y t d a h u r   _Thursday_

2 t e u y a s d   _____

3 d i a f r y   _____

4 o n d m a y   _____

5 a u d a r y t s   _____

6 e e d w d a s n y   _____

7 a y n d s u   _____

SELF CHECK   Now I can ...

☐ say the days of the week

☐ tell the time

☐ talk about places at different times

1

HELLO!

Friends hug to say hello in New York, the United States.

PREVIEW

A **Complete the conversation.** Use the words in the box.

> Hi   I'm   spell   Bye   name   What's

Kate: Hello. ¹ _____ Kate. ² _____ your name?

Rob: ³ _____ , Kate. My ⁴ _____ is Rob.

Kate: How do you ⁵ _____ that?

Rob: R-O-B

Kate: Bye, Rob.

Rob: ⁶ _____ , Kate.

B **Write the missing words in 1–4.** Use ***am***, ***is***, or ***are***. Then rewrite the sentences using contractions.

I ¹ _____ *am* _____ Stig.	⁵ *I'm Stig.*
She ² _____ Maya.	⁶
He ³ _____ Ming.	⁷
You ⁴ _____ Nadine.	⁸

LANGUAGE FOCUS

A Write questions and answers.

1 A: _____What's his name?_____

   B: _____His name is Ming._____

3 A: _____

   B: _____

2 A: _____

   B: _____

4 A: _____

   B: _____

B Join the letters of the alphabet in the correct order.

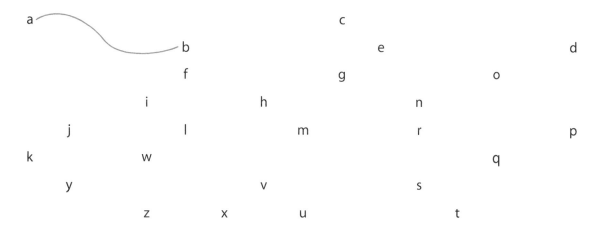

C Rewrite the conversation with the correct capital letters.

1 **A:** hi. my name's rosa. what's your name?   _____

   _____

   B: hello. i'm michael.   _____

2 **A:** bye, rosa.   _____

   B: bye, michael.   _____

GREETINGS

Label the photos. Use the words in the box.

> bow   fist bump   hug   kiss   shake hands   wave

1 _____

4 _____

2 _____

5 _____

3 _____

6 _____

VOCABULARY

A Complete the labels.

1 My ___family___ .

2 _____ . _____ Tom.

3 _____ . _____ Sophie.

4 ___My mom.___ . ___Her name is___ Emma.

5 _____ . _____ Lucas.

6 Me

B Match.

1 ○   ○ pen

2 ○   ○ chair

3 ○   ○ book

4 ○   ○ eraser

5 ○   ○ computer

6 ○   ○ pencil

C Find the words in the box. Circle the items in the picture.

| Maya's chair | Nadine's chair | Nadine's computer | Maya's book |
| Ming's eraser | Stig's desk | Ming's pen | Stig's paper |

A group of girls paint a wall during a festival in Lebanon.

2

WHERE ARE YOU FROM?

PREVIEW

A Rearrange the letters to make colors.

1 rnwbo ___brown___

2 eihwt _____

3 rde _____

4 oelywl _____

5 pnki _____

6 ckabl _____

7 elub _____

8 neraog _____

9 egner _____

10 ruppel _____

B Complete the crossword puzzle.

Across: 2 ■, 3 ■, 5 ■, 6 ■, 8 ■, 9 ☐. **Down:** 1 ■, 3 ■, 4 ■, 7 ■.

LANGUAGE FOCUS

A Complete the conversation. Write questions and answers.

José, Mexico

Wendy, China

Hiroshi and Takako, Japan

1 A: Where's José from?   **B:** He's from Mexico.

2 A: _____ Wendy _____ ?

    B: _____ .

3 A: _____ Hiroshi and Takako _____ ?

    B: _____ .

B Complete the word search. Find six different countries.

H	E	J	J	A	P	A	N	O	T	G	G	F	K
K	S	O	U	T	H	A	F	R	I	C	A	S	Q
B	R	A	Z	I	L	O	J	S	W	E	D	E	N
E	U	Y	Y	T	U	R	K	E	Y	S	Z	J	N
P	A	U	S	T	R	A	L	I	A	W	Q	A	X

C Complete the chart. Write the countries from **B** and their nationalities.

Country	Nationality
Japan	Japanese

Country	Nationality

D Complete the sentences. Write *a* or *an*.

1 It's ___*a*___ board.   **3** It's _____ eraser.   **5** It's _____ blue pencil.

2 It's _____ orange pen.   **4** It's _____ desk.   **6** It's _____ computer.

FLAGS

Flags flying in front of the European Parliament in Brussels, Belgium.

Read the sentences. Write the countries.

- Peru's flag is red and white.
- Pakistan's flag is green and white.
- Finland's flag is blue and white.
- Bulgaria's flag is red, green, and white.
- Germany's flag is red, black, and yellow.
- Malaysia's flag is red, white, blue, and yellow.

1 _____

4 _____

2 _____

5 _____

3 _____

6 _____

VOCABULARY

A **Label the pictures.** Use the words in the box.

> ball   fast   player   strong   the winner   the world

1 _____

3 _____

5 _____

2 _____

4 baseball _____

6 _____

B **Label the continents.**

1 North America _____

2 _____

3 _____

4 _____

5 _____

6 _____

7 _____

C **Write the countries.** Use the words in the box.

> Brazil   Canada   China   South Africa   Spain   Sweden

1 _____ is in Asia.

2 _____ is in South America.

3 _____ is in Africa.

4 _____ is in North America.

5 _____ and _____ are in Europe.

3

WHAT'S
THAT?

A man holds his pet hedgehog.

PREVIEW

What are these animals? Label the photos. Use the words in the box.

rabbit   fish   dog   bird   cat   mouse

1 _____

3 _____

5 _____

2 _____

4 _____

6 _____

LANGUAGE FOCUS

A **Complete the conversations.** Circle the correct words.

Grace: What's [1] **this / those**?

Tomas: [2] **They're / It's** my bird.

Grace: What are [3] **that / these**?

Tomas: [4] **They're / It's** mice.

Grace: What are [5] **that / those**?

Tomas: [6] **They're / It's** rabbits.

B **Rearrange the words to make conversations.**

1 **A:** this / What's _____?

   B: a / It's / pen _____.

   A: Is / it / pen / your _____?

   B: is / it / Yes, _____.

2 **A:** are / those / What _____?

   B: books / They're _____.

   A: Are / books / they / your _____?

   B: books / Melissa's / No, / they're _____.

C **Complete the questions and answers.**

1 **A:** What's ___*that*___ ?

   B: ___*It's*___ an eraser.

3 **A:** What are _____ ?

   B: _____ books.

2 **A:** What are _____ ?

   B: _____ pens.

4 **A:** What's _____ ?

   B: _____ a pencil.

Five golden snub-nosed monkeys in China

A Complete the words. Use the chart. Then number the pictures 1–4.

one	two	three	four	five	six	seven	eight	nine	ten	eleven	twelve
b	y	g	t	a	d	z	u	c	l	i	r

1 ____ ____ ____ ____ ____ ____
    10   7   5   12

2 ____ ____ ____ ____ ____
       5   1   11

3 ____ ____ ____
    9

4 ____ ____ ____ ____ ____ ____ ____
    10   6 2   8   3

 a ____

 b ____

 c ____

 d ____

B Write the missing numbers in words.

1 ten – eight = _____

2 one + _____ = eleven

3 three × four = _____

4 two × _____ = ten

5 seven – three = _____

6 four × two = _____

90 Unit 3

VOCABULARY

A Label the pictures. Use the words in the box.

> tongue   long   eat   tree   change   eyes

1 _____

3 _____

5 _____

2 _____

4 _____

6 _____

B Complete the crossword with the plural form of these words.

Across:

2 mouse

4 woman

6 sheep

Down:

1 book

2 man

3 child

5 fish

7 pen

4

IT'S A CELEBRATION!

A boy celebrates his birthday with his family in Shanghai, China.

PREVIEW

A Rearrange the letters to make birthday words.

1 akce   ____ ____ ____ ____

2 dcra   ____ ____ ____ ____

3 gitf   ____ ____ ____ ____

4 yrapt   ____ ____ ____ ____ ____

5 nlaced   ____ ____ ____ ____ ____ ____

6 noblalo   ____ ____ ____ ____ ____ ____ ____

B Write the words in the crossword puzzle.

Across:

3 🎈

5 🎂

6 🎁

Down:

1 🕯️

2 💌

4 🙌

LANGUAGE FOCUS

A **Complete the conversation.** Circle the correct words.

Sara: What [1] **date** / **month** is it today?

Danny: It's July 9th.

Sara: [2] **When** / **What** is your birthday?

Danny: It's July 10th.

Sara: So your birthday is [3] **today** / **tomorrow**!

Danny: Yes, it is! When's your birthday?

Sara: It's April 1st.

Danny: Oh! That's April Fools' Day!

B **Rearrange the letters.** Write the months of the year. Then number the months 1 to 12.

a __8__ tAugsu   _A_ _u_ _g_ _u_ _s_ _t_

b _____ cahMr   ___ ___ ___ ___ ___

c _____ unJraay   ___ ___ ___ ___ ___ ___ ___

d _____ eunJ   ___ ___ ___ ___

e _____ Fruyarbe   ___ ___ ___ ___ ___ ___ ___ ___

f _____ meeSbrept   ___ ___ ___ ___ ___ ___ ___ ___ ___

g _____ yMa   ___ ___ ___

h _____ pilrA   ___ ___ ___ ___ ___

i _____ emovrNbe   ___ ___ ___ ___ ___ ___ ___ ___

j _____ ebrctoO   ___ ___ ___ ___ ___ ___ ___

k _____ ulJy   ___ ___ ___ ___

l _____ ercbDeme   ___ ___ ___ ___ ___ ___ ___ ___

C **Find the patterns.** Write the numbers in words.

1 nineteen   twenty   _twenty-one_   twenty-two

2 twelve   fourteen   _____   eighteen

3 forty-two   thirty-nine   thirty-six   _____

4 ninety   eighty   seventy   _____

5 _____   forty-two   fifty-four   sixty-six

A forest in winter in Bosnia and Hercegovina

A   Write the seasons.

1 _____

3 _____

2 _____

4 _____

B   Complete the seasons. Then look at the chart for Tokyo, Japan, and write the months for each season.

seasons	sp _____	su _____
months		
seasons	fa _____	wi _____
months		

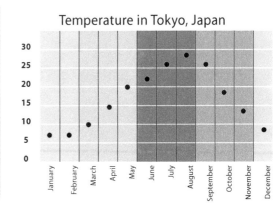

Temperature in Tokyo, Japan

VOCABULARY

A Complete the sentences. Circle the correct words.

In photo 1, three [1] **friends / blankets** are enjoying a [2] **flower / picnic**. Their [3] **park / blanket** is
on the [4] **friends / ground**. Photo 2 is a picture of a beautiful [5] **park / blanket**. The [6] **flowers /
picnics** are red and yellow.

B Complete the puzzle to find the secret word. Use the clues below.

1 December is the _____ month.

2 _____ is the first month.

3 _____ is the third month.

4 April is the _____ month.

5 _____ is the ninth month.

6 November is the _____ month.

The secret word is _____ .

C Complete the chart.

fifteenth		twentieth			31st	sixty-fifth	
	18th		22nd	fifty-sixth		eighty-second	
nineteenth		twenty-eighth			43rd		97th

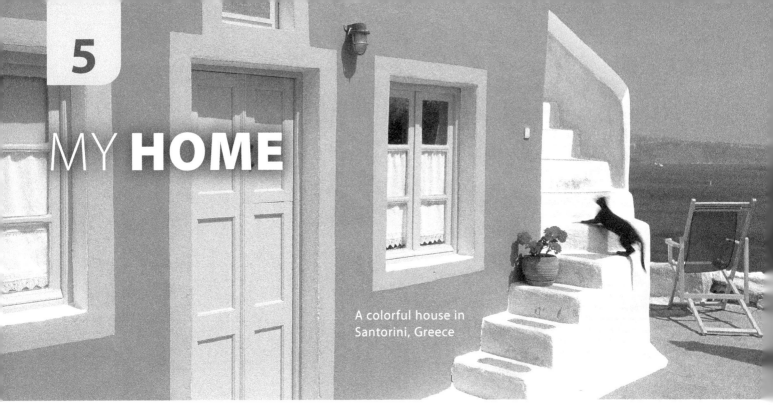

A colorful house in Santorini, Greece

5 MY HOME

PREVIEW

A **Complete the places in a house.** Use the chart.

a	b	d	g	k	n	t	v	y
eleven	twenty-two	thirty-three	forty-four	fifty-five	sixty-six	seventy-seven	eighty-eight	ninety-nine

1 __b__ ____ ____ ____ ____ ____ ____ ____
  22   11

2 ____ ____ ____ ____ ____ ____   ____ ____ ____
        88   66   44

3 ____ ____ ____ ____ ____ ____
  22   33

4 ____ ____ ____ ____
  99 11

5 ____ ____ ____ ____ ____ ____
  55   77   66

B **Complete the sentences.** Use the words from **A**.

1 The apple is in the _____ .

2 The bed is in the _____ .

3 The TV is in the _____ .

4 The tree is in the _____ .

5 The bath is in the _____ .

LANGUAGE FOCUS

A **Write questions using the words in parentheses.** Then match the questions to the answers.

1 (TV / living room)

_____*Is the TV in the living room*_____ ? ○   ○ **a** No, they aren't.

2 (where / TV)

_____*Where's the TV*_____ ? ○   ○ **b** Yes, it is.

3 (trees / bedroom)

_____ ? ○   ○ **c** They're in the bedroom.

4 (bed / kitchen)

_____ ? ○   ○ **d** It's in the living room.

5 (where / books)

_____ ? ○   ○ **e** No, it isn't.

B **Look at the photos.** Answer the questions.

1 Is the woman in the yard?

_____ .

2 Where are the cats?

_____ .

3 Is the computer in the kitchen?

_____ .

4 Is the boy in the bedroom?

_____ .

5 Is the bed in the house?

_____ .

THE REAL WORLD

A dinosaur fossil in a house in
Louisiana, the United States

A **Rearrange the words.** Make questions about the photo.

1 Are / bedroom / boys / in / the / the

_____ *Are the boys in the bedroom* _____ ?

2 dog / in / Is / the / the / yard

_____ ?

3 dinosaurs' / head / house / in / Is / the / the

_____ ?

4 bathroom / boys' / in / Is / mom / the / the

_____ ?

5 and / Are / boys' / dad / house / in / mom / the / the

_____ ?

B **Write answers to the questions in A.**

1 _____ *No, they aren't* _____ .

2 _____ .

3 _____ .

4 _____ .

5 _____ .

VOCABULARY

A **Rearrange the letters to make words from the reading passage on page 63.**

1 hiuocns   ____ ____ ____ ____ ____ ____ ____

2 evtos   ____ ____ ____ ____ ____

3 hucoc   ____ ____ ____ ____ ____

4 sitasr   ____ ____ ____ ____ ____

5 dinwwo   ____ ____ ____ ____ ____

B **Label the photo.** Use the words in the box.

> hand   eye   hair   arm   leg   foot   nose

A man walking on a rope in Rio de Janeiro, Brazil.

1 _____

2 _____

3 _____

4 _____

5 _____

6 _____

7 _____

6

WHAT TIME IS IT?

Workers clean
Big Ben's clock face
in London, England

PREVIEW

Complete the crossword.

Across:

1 10 a.m. and 4 p.m. are in the _____.

3 6:30 p.m. is in the _____.

5 9 a.m. is in the _____.

Down:

2 4 p.m. is in the _____.

4 11 p.m. and 3 a.m. are at _____.

LANGUAGE FOCUS

A **Match the times and expressions.**

1 It's 11:30 p.m. ○   ○ **a** Good afternoon.

2 It's 4:00 p.m. ○   ○ **b** Good night.

3 It's 8:00 a.m. ○   ○ **c** Good evening.

4 It's 7:30 p.m. ○   ○ **d** Good morning.

B **What time is it?** Write the times.

1 _eight fifteen_

4 _____

2 _____

5 _____

3 _____

6 _____

C **Complete the conversation.** Rearrange the words.

Ana: morning / Good   1 _____ .

Yuki: Hi, / up / what's   2 _____ ?

Ana: is / it / time / What   3 _____ ?

Yuki: eight / It's / thirty   4 _____ .

Ana: day / is / it / What   5 _____ ?

Yuki: Tuesday / It's   6 _____ .

Ana: you / Thank   7 _____ .

THE REAL WORLD

Bike lanes at night
in Sao Paulo, Brazil

A **Look at the chart.** Answer the questions.

Los Angeles	−8	4 a.m.
New York	−5	7 a.m.
Sao Paulo	−3	9 a.m.
London	0	12 p.m.
Cape Town	+2	2 p.m.
Singapore	+8	8 p.m.
Sydney	+10	10 p.m.

1 It's 8 p.m. in London. What time is it in Singapore? _It's 4 a.m._

2 It's 7 a.m. in London. What time is it in Sydney? _____

3 It's 3 p.m. in London. What time is it in Cape Town? _____

4 It's 4 a.m. in London. What time is it in New York? _____

B **Write these numbers in words.**

1 2,000 _____

2 3,000,000 _____

3 5,000,000,000 _____

VOCABULARY

A **Label the photos.** Use the words in the box.

> bell   tourists   model   clock   city   a show

1 _____

4 _____

2 _____

5 _____

3 _____

6 _____

B **Write the correct days.**

1 Monday, _____, Wednesday

2 Friday, Saturday, _____

3 Sunday, _____, Tuesday

4 Wednesday, _____, Friday

VOCABULARY

LANGUAGE NOTES

UNIT 1 HELLO!

AM / IS / ARE (*TO BE* SINGULAR)	
I'm Stig. **You're** Nadine. **She's** Maya. **He's** Ming.	
HIS / HER / YOUR / MY (POSSESSIVE ADJECTIVES)	
What's **your** name? What's **his** name? What's **her** name? What's **my** name?	**My** name is Stig. **His** name is Ming. **Her** name is Maya. **Your** name is Nadine.
'S (POSSESSIVE S)	
Maya**'s** family name is Santos.	

UNIT 2 WHERE ARE YOU FROM?

TALKING ABOUT YOUR COUNTRY (USING *FROM* AND NATIONALITIES)		
Where are you **from**? **Where's** he **from**? **Where** are you **from**? **Where** are they **from**?	I'm **from** He's **from** We're **from** They're **from**	Brazil. I'm **Brazilian**. Japan. He's **Japanese**. the United States. We're **American**. Korea. They're **Korean**.
OUR / YOUR / THEIR (POSSESSIVE ADJECTIVES)		
Our / **Your** / **Their**	names are	Nadine and Maya.
ASKING ABOUT COLORS		
What color is it?	It's green / red / blue.	

UNIT 3 WHAT'S THAT?

THIS / THAT / THESE / THOSE (DEMONSTRATIVES)			
What's this?	**It's** a dog.	**What are these?**	**They're** cats.
What's that?	**It's** a spider.	**What are those?**	**They're** rabbits.
A / AN (ARTICLES)			
a cat		an eraser	
SINGULAR AND PLURAL			
cat		cat**s**	
pen		pen**s**	

UNIT 4 IT'S A CELEBRATION!

TALKING ABOUT DATES AND AGES	
How old are you?	I'm 15 years old.
How old is he?	He's 32 years old.
It isn't his birthday.	
He isn't 25 years old.	
What's the date?	It's August 5th.
When's your birthday?	It's January 8th.
What month is it?	It's January / February / March …

UNIT 5 MY HOME

TALKING ABOUT WHERE THINGS ARE (USING THE VERB *BE* WITH *WHERE* AND *IN*)	
Where is the dog? **Where are** the books?	**It's in** the yard. **They're in** the living room.
Is the dog **in** the yard?	Yes, he **is**. No, he **isn't**.
Are the books **in** the kitchen?	Yes, they **are**. No, they **aren't**.

UNIT 6 WHAT TIME IS IT?

TALKING ABOUT TIME AND DAYS	
What time is it?	It's 8 o'clock. (8:00) It's nine thirty. (9:30) It's eight forty-five. (8:45) It's ten oh eight. (10:08) It's 10 a.m. (10:00) It's 6 p.m. (6:00)
Good morning. / Good afternoon./ Good evening. / Good night.	

CREDITS

Photo Credits
Cover AirPano.com, **4** (from top to bottom) recep–bg/E+/Getty Images; ABC Photo Archives/Walt Disney Television/Getty Images; James Caldwell/Alamy Stock Photo; Jeremy Woodhouse/Blend Images/Getty Images; Horizon International Images Limited/Alamy Stock Photo; Anatoleya/Moment/Getty Images, **7** MachineHeadz/iStock/Getty Images, **8–9** (spread) recep–bg/E+/Getty Images, **11** (c) Hero Images Inc./Alamy Stock Photo; (br) Dragan Milovanovic/Shutterstock.com, **12** (t) Fred R. Conrad/The New York Times/Redux; (cr) Makkuro GL/Shutterstock.com; (c) Leremy/Shutterstock.com; (cr) Leremy/Shutterstock.com; (bl) Martial Red/Shutterstock.com; (br) Martial Red/Shutterstock.com, **13** (b) Westend61/Getty Images, **14–15** (spread) mixetto/E+/Getty Images, **15** (t) (c1) (c2) (b) mixetto/E+/Getty Images, **16** (t) Hill Street Studios/DigitalVision/Getty Images, **17** (t) You Touch Pix of EuToch/Shutterstock.com; (b1) aldomurillo/iStock/Getty Images; (b2) Dragan Milovanovic/Shutterstock.com; (c1) (c2) (c3) (c4) © Cengage 2020; (c5) Puckung/Shutterstock.com; (c6) Emmeewhite/Shutterstock.com; (c7) VikiVector/Shutterstock.com; (c8) vectorisland/Shutterstock.com, **18–19** (b) Thomas Barwick/Image Bank Film: Signature/Getty Images, **19** (c) AlexHliv/Shutterstock.com; (b1) © Cengage 2020; (b2) © Cengage 2020; (b3) © Cengage 2020; (b4) © Cengage 2020, **20–21** (Spread) ABC Photo Archives/Walt Disney Television/Getty Images, **23** (tl) FG Trade/E+/Getty Images; (cl) Chalffy/E+/Getty Images; (tr) Blend Images - KidStock/DigitalVision/Getty Images, **23** (cr) hsyncoban/iStock/Getty Images; (b) Marco Rubino/EyeEm/Getty Images, **24** (cl) (cr) (bl) (br) Ints Vikmanis/Shutterstock.com; (t) EduLeite/E+/Getty Images, **25** (tl) (tc1) (tr) (tc2) Ints Vikmanis/Shutterstock.com, **26–27** (Spread) AP Images/Marijan Murat, **28** (b) © Cengage 2020; (tl) Jon Feingersh/Iconica/Getty Images; (tc) Srdjan Randjelovic/Shutterstock.com; (tr) Atakan Yildiz/Shutterstock.com; (cl) strickke/E+/Getty Images; (c) Radius Images/Alamy Stock Photo; (cr) Fuse/Corbis/Getty Images, **29** (c) Sidhe/Shutterstock.com; (br1) Dragan Milovanovic/Shutterstock.com; (br2) Clive Mason/Getty Images Sport/Getty Images, **30–31** (Spread) Matthew Stockman/Getty Images Sport/Getty Images, **32–33** (Spread) James Caldwell/Alamy Stock Photo, **33** (tc) (tr) bioraven/Shutterstock.com; (cl) (c) (cr) Alexandr III/Shutterstock.com; (tl) Kilroy79/Shutterstock.com, **36** (t) Klein and Hubert/Minden Pictures, **37** (b) SolStock/E+/Getty Images, **38–39** (Spread) Nick Garbutt/NPL/Minden Pictures, **40** (t) MyImages - Micha/Shutterstock.com, **41** (tl) Jenny Sturm/Shutterstock.com; (tr) br) monkeybusinessimages/iStock/Getty Images; (cl) Georgette Douwma/Photographer's Choice/Getty Images; (cr) Rawpixel/iStock/Getty Images; (bl) tiripero/iStock/Getty Images; (b) Steve Tum/Shutterstock.com, **42–43** (b) Joel Sartore/National Geographic Photo Ark/National Geographic Image Collection, **43** (tl) Larry-Rains/Shutterstock.com; (cl) tantri01/Shutterstock.com; (cr) vtaurus/Shutterstock.com; (tr) (bl) (br) Alexandr III/Shutterstock.com, **44–45** (Spread) Jeremy Woodhouse/Blend Images/Getty Images, **45** (tl) Best Vector Elements/Shutterstock.com; (tr) Puckung/Shutterstock.com; (cl) Mr.Creative/Shutterstock.com; (bl) Gisele Yashar/Shutterstock.com; (br) Rashad Ashur/Shutterstock.com, **47** (t) iperion/Shutterstock.com; (br) Michael Weber/imageBROKER/Alamy Stock Photo, **48** (t) Helminadia/Moment/Getty Images; (cl) (c1) (c2) (c3) lettett/Shutterstock.com, **49** (b) Rawpixel.com/Shutterstock.com, **50–51** (Spread) Pierre Ogeron/Moment/Getty Images, **52** (Spread) ChameleonsEye/Shutterstock.com; (tl) vinhdav/Getty Images; (tr) Mostlysunny/Shutterstock.com; (cr) Ihor Hvozdetskyi/Shutterstock.com; (c) Relaximages/Alamy Stock Photo; (tc) C. Devan/Corbis/Getty Images, **53** (tl) fotogestoeber/Shutterstock.com; (tr) Viktor Jarema/Shutterstock.com; (br) John S Lander/LightRocket/Getty Images; (b) Dragan Milovanovic/Shutterstock.com, **54** (tl) Nuno Valadas/iStock/Getty Images; (tc) powerofforever/E+/Getty Images; (tr) Indian Food Images/Shutterstock.com, **54–55** (Spread) Srikanth Varma/EyeEm/Getty Images, **56–57** (Spread) Horizon International Images Limited/Alamy Stock Photo, **57** (tl) (tr) (cr) (bl) bioraven/Shutterstock.com; (cl) graphixmania/Shutterstock.com; (br) BestVectorIcon/Shutterstock.com, **60** (t) (cl) (cr) (bc) Gabriele Galimberti and Juri Di Luca/National Geographic Image Collection, **62–63** (Spread) Guillaume Dutilh @PhotoXplorer, **63** (t) HamsterMan/Shutterstock.com; (b) Carlos E. Santa Maria/Shutterstock.com, **65** (t) LeighSmithImages/Alamy Stock Photo; (c) Lars Hallström/age fotostock/Getty Images; (br1) mixetto/E+/Getty Images; (br2) natrot/Shutterstock.com, **66** (cl) szaffy/iStock/Getty Images; (c) Agencja Fotograficzna Caro/Alamy Stock Photo; (tc) Ferrari/ZUMA Press/Newscom; (tl) Uwe Aranas/Shutterstock.com; (cr) Dino Geromella/Shutterstock.com; (tr) Sandra Foyt/Shutterstock.com, **66–67** (Spread) Gilles Targat/Photo 12/Alamy Stock Photo, **67** (cl) (c) (cr) (bc) (b) bsd/Shutterstock.com; (bl) Deemak Daksina/Shutterstock.com, **68–69** (Spread) Anatoleya/Moment/Getty Images, **69** (tl) (tr) (cl) (cr) (bl) Kurdanfell/Shutterstock.com; (br) urbazon/E+/Getty Images, **72** (t) Cris Faga/NurPhoto/Getty Images, **73** (tl) (cl) (cr) ©John Stanmeyer, **74** (tc) mesteban75/iStock/Getty Images, **74–75** Nenad Nedomacki/Shutterstock.com, **76** (tl) ChrisHepburn/E+/Getty Images; (tr) PR Image Factory/Shutterstock.com; (cl) Peter Nadolski/Shutterstock.com; (bl) Jakub.it/Shutterstock.com; (br) CactusPilot/Shutterstock.com; (cr) Otar Gujejiani/Shutterstock.com, **77** (tr) Anna Kucherova/Shutterstock.com; (tl) Viktor Jarema/Shutterstock.com; (br) Seqoya/iStock/Getty Images; (b) GreenLandStudio/Shutterstock.com, **78–79** (spread) OGphoto/E+/Getty Images, **79** (tl) (tr) (cl) (cr) ARM stockers/Shutterstock.com, **80** (t) Erica Shires/Corbis/Getty Images, **82** (cl1) recep–bg/E+/Getty Images; (cr1) SDI Productions/E+/Getty Images; (cl2) Rido/Shutterstock.com; (cr2) Mikael Vaisanen/Corbis/Getty Images; (bl) piranka/E+/Getty Images; (br) Kohei Hara/DigitalVision/Getty Images; (tl) Odilon Dimier/PhotoAlto/Getty Images, **83** (t) ferrantraite/E+/Getty Images, **84** (t) ANWAR AMRO/AFP/Getty Images, **85** (tl) Jose Luis Pelaez Inc/DigitalVision/Getty Images; (tc) Carlina Teteris/Moment/Getty Images; (tr) UFO RF/amana images/Getty Images, **86** (t) AdrianHancu/iStock/Getty Images; (cl) (cr) (bl) (br) Ints Vikmanis/Shutterstock.com, **87** (tl) Artsiom Petrushenka/Shutterstock.com; (cl) aapsky/Shutterstock.com; (tc) Billion Photos/Shutterstock.com; (c) Matt_Brown/E+/Getty Images; (tr) Oleksandr Zamuruiev/Shutterstock.com; (cr) ERproductions Ltd/Blend Images; (b) © Cengage 2020, **88** (t) Kamonrat Meunklad/EyeEm/Getty Images; (cl) Dorottya Mathe/Shutterstock.com; (c) Maly Designer/Shutterstock.com; (cr) Ferenc zelepcsenyi/Shutterstock.com; (bl) CreativeNature_nl/iStock/Getty Images; (bc) Denis Tabler/Shutterstock.com; (br) astock/Shutterstock.com, **89** (br) Denis Tabler/Shutterstock.com, **90** (t) Thomas Marent/Minden Pictures; (c1)Kilroy79/Shutterstock.com; (c2) Rvector/Shutterstock.com; (c3) bioraven/Shutterstock.com; (c4) tantri01/Shutterstock.com, **91** (tl) Baranov E/Shutterstock.com; (tr) sezer66/Shutterstock.com; (c) Alexander Kirch/Shutterstock.com; (tc) MelindaChan/Moment/Getty Images; (cl) Manuela Durson/Shutterstock.com; (cr) Daniel Day/Stone/Getty Images, **92** (t) John Stanmeyer; (cr1) Gisele Yashar/Shutterstock.com; (cl2) Best Vector Elements/Shutterstock.com; (cl1) Rashad Ashur/Shutterstock.com; (cr2) Puckung/Shutterstock.com; (bl) Mr.Creative/Shutterstock.com, **94** (t) Adnan Bubalo/500px/Getty Images; (cr) (cl) (br) (bl) lettett/Shutterstock.com, **95** (tl) Daniela Buoncristiani/Cultura/Getty Images; (tr) Dmitry Rukhlenko/Shutterstock.com, **96** (t) Gavin Hellier/Robert Harding Library, **97** (cl) Image Source/Alamy Stock Photo; (cr) Chris Gramly/Getty Images, **98** (t) Gabriele Galimberti and Juri Di Luca/National Geographic Image Collection, **99** (b) Keith Ladzinski/National Geographic Image Collection, **100** (t) Stephen Hird/REUTERS, **101** (c) ARM stockers/Shutterstock.com, **102** (t) Bambu Productions/DigitalVision/Getty Images, **103** (cl) Niklebedev/Shutterstock.com; (bl) Drazen_/E+/Getty Images; (br) FooTToo/Shutterstock.com; (tl) HemantMandot/iStock/Getty Images; (tr)Tom Kelley Archive/Retrofile/Getty Images; (cr) georgeclerk/iStock Unreleased/Getty Images

Art Credits
5, 10, 22, 34, 35, 46, 58, 70, 81, 83 (b), **89** (b) Ed Hammond/Deborah Wolfe Ltd, **6, 17** (t), **59, 61** Peter Bull Art Studio

ACKNOWLEDGMENTS

Thank you to the educators who provided invaluable feedback during the development of *Time Zones*:

ADVISORS

Apryl Peredo, Teacher, Hongo Junior and Senior High School, Tokyo
Carolina Espinosa, Coordinator, Associação Cultural Brasil-Estados Unidos, Brazil
Chary Aguirre, Academic and English Coordinator, Colegio Muñoz, Mexico
Elizabeth Yonetsugi, Global Program Manager, Berlitz Japan, Tokyo
Helena Mesquita Bizzarri, Academic Coordinator, SESI, Brazil
Hiroyo Noguchi, Lecturer, Momoyama Gakuin University (St. Andrew's University), Osaka
Isabella Alvim, Academic Coordinator, Instituto Brasil-Estados Unidos (IBEU) - Rio de Janeiro, Brazil
Kota Ikeshima, Teacher, Shibuya Junior & Senior High School, Tokyo
Nelly Romero, Head of Academic Design and Projects, Instituto Cultural Peruano Norteamericano (ICPNA), Peru
Nhi Nguyen, Program Manager, Vietnam USA Society English Centers (VUS), Ho Chi Minh City
Sabrina Hong, Education and Training Manager, Aston English, Xi'an
Sean Patterson, Global Programs Manager, Kanto Gakuin Mutsuura Junior and Senior High School, Yokohama
Sílvia de Melo Caldas, Course Designer, Casa Thomas Jefferson, Brazil
Sophy Oum, Academic Coordinator, ACE Cambodia, Phnom Penh
Wenjing Luo, Research and Development Manager, CERNET Education, Beijing
Yu-Chih (Portia) Chang, Head Teacher, Start Education Experts, Taipei

REVIEWERS

LATIN AMERICA

Adriene Zigaib, Brazil
Ana Paula Marques Migliari, School Connect, Brazil
Anna Lúcia Seabra Mendes, Casa Thomas Jefferson, Brazil
Auricea Bacelar, Top Seven Idiomas, Brazil
Barbara Souza, EM Maria Quiteria, Brazil
Daniela Coelho, SayOk! English School, Brazil
Gilberto Dalla Verde Junior, Colégio Tomas Agostinho, Brazil
Isabella Campos, Instituto Brasil-Estados Unidos (IBEU) - Rio de Janeiro, Brazil
Jessica Yanett Carrillo Torres, John Nash School, Peru
Juliana Pinho, Instituto Brasil-Estados Unidos (IBEU), Brazil
Juliana Ribeiro Lima Passos, CIEP 117 Carlos Drummond de Andrade Brasil-USA, Brazil
Katherin Ortiz Torres, Santa Angela Merici School, Peru
Kathleen Isabelle Tavares da Silva, Inglês Para Todos, Brazil
Larissa Pizzano Platinetti Vieira, Centro Cultural Brasil - Estados Unidos (CCBEU) Guarapuava, Brazil
Laura Raffo Pires, Extra English, Brazil
Luis Sergio Moreira da Silva, Webster, Brazil
María del Rosario Aguirre Román, Colegio Muñoz, Mexico
Maria Helena Querioz e Lima, Cultura Inglesa Uberlândia, Brazil
Mónica Rosales, Instituto Franklin de Veracruz, Mexico
Natasha Freitas Silva, ATW English, Brazil
Natasha Pereira, ATW English, Brazil
Neri Zabdi Barrenechea Garcia, Welcome English, Peru
Patricia Perez, Colégio Martin Miguel de Guemes, Argentina
Raphael Fonseca Porto, Casa Thomas Jefferson, Brazil
Renata Lucia Cardoso, Instituto Natural de Desenvolvimento Infantil, Brazil
Roosevelt Oliveira, Coopling, Brazil
Samuel Nicacio Silva Santos, Casa Thomas Jefferson, Brazil
Silvia Castilho Cintra, Ingles com Silvia, Brazil
Silvia Martínez Marín, I.E.P. Henri La Fontaine, Peru
Stela Foley, Brazil

EUROPE AND AFRICA

Theresa Taylor, American Language Center, Morocco

ASIA

Andrew Duenas, ILA Vietnam, Ho Chi Minh City
Camille Nota, Berlitz Japan, Tokyo
Dan Quinn, Jakarta Japanese School, Jakarta
Edwin G Wiehe, Shitennoji Junior and Senior High School, Osaka
Georges Erhard, ILA Vietnam, Ho Chi Minh City
Haruko Morimoto, Kanda Gaigo Career College, Tokyo
Mai Thị Ngọc Anh, ILA Vietnam, Ho Chi Minh City
Masaki Aso, Japan University of Economics, Fukuoka
Paul Adams, Ming Dao High School, Taichung
Samuel Smith, Jakarta Japanese School, Jakarta
Sayidah Salim, Dian Didatika Junior High School, Jakarta
Shogo Minagawa, Doshisha Junior High School, Kyoto
Trevor Goodwin, IBL English, Wonju
Yoko Sakurai, Aichi University, Nagoya